LIFE
DEATH
JUDGMENT
&
ETERNITY

GEORGE E PFAUTSCH

authorHOUSE®

AuthorHouse™
1663 Liberty Drive
Bloomington, IN 47403
www.authorhouse.com
Phone: 833-262-8899

Published by AuthorHouse 06/23/2022

ISBN: 978-1-6655-6351-2 (sc)
ISBN: 978-1-6655-6350-5 (e)

Library of Congress Control Number: 2022911593

Print information available on the last page.

Any people depicted in stock imagery provided by Getty Images are models, and such images are being used for illustrative purposes only. Certain stock imagery © Getty Images.

Scriptural passages have been taken from The New American Bible - St. Joseph Edition and all catechetical passages have been taken from the Catechism of the Catholic Church.

This book is printed on acid-free paper.

CONTENTS

ETERNITY

INTRODUCTION

Life, death, judgment and eternity are certainties that all human beings will face. In a humanistic world it is an unfortunate truth that many humans ignore all those certainties, except life. When ignoring those certainties, humans are also prone to focus on that which brings success in life but not in death, judgment or eternity.

Our life on earth is a struggle. God made humans in his own image and likeness. But God also gave humans a free will. That free will was given to the first humans on earth; Adam and Eve. God put them to the test of choosing good or evil when He gave them the Garden of Eden for their dwelling place on earth. He gave them one commandment. They were not allowed to eat the fruit of the forbidden tree. But when tempted by the devil they broke that commandment and ate of the forbidden fruit. From that point forward, humans have been born with the original sin of pride, which in turn leads to other sins.

If God in his perfect wisdom knew that humans would sin against his commandments, it is a fair question to ask why God created humans. In his great love for humans, he wanted them to share in his eternal and blessed life. In order to demonstrate his great love for his human creations, He also sent his only begotten Son to earth to suffer and die so the sins of humans would be forgiven. Yes, God created humans so they would one day share in his magnificent kingdom, but he left it to the free will of humans to decide for themselves if they wished to one day live eternally in that Kingdom.

It is through love that God created humans. What He expects of humans is a reciprocation of that love. Our life on earth is a trial to test the degree of that love. He does not force us to love Him but gave us many ways to demonstrate that love. Through the prophets of the Old Testament and especially through his Son he has revealed to us his expectations. How we live our life on earth in fulfillment of those expectations, ultimately determines our place in his eternal Kingdom.

Because our life on earth determines our place in eternity, it seems that wisdom would dictate a life that focuses on obtaining an eternal life of bliss. As long ago as the time the Old Testament was written we were told that fear of God is the foundation of wisdom. We are foolish when we think otherwise. We are also sinners when we believe otherwise. It is the wise human who understands that it is God who needs to be the focus of our life. When God is the focus of our life, we need not fear our place in eternity.

The purpose of this book is to provide the reader with reminders of all the certainties human beings must one day face. It will focus on things we must do on earth to live this life as God would have us live it, but it will also note the things humans must avoid during their life on earth.

This book will also examine the consequences of how humans live their lives on earth. We will rely heavily on Sacred Scriptures and Apostolic Tradition as we also review death, judgment and eternity.

LIFE

CHAPTER 1

WHY GOD MADE HUMANS

When the Baltimore Catechism was the standard text for teaching Catholic elementary age students, the 3rd question of that text asked, "Why Did God Make us"? In the current edition of the New St. Joseph Baltimore Catechism # 1 the answer is given as follows; "God made us to show forth His goodness and to share with us His everlasting happiness in heaven".

The following question in that edition of the Baltimore Catechism asks and tells us that if we wish to gain eternal happiness, "we must know, love and serve God in this world". How we are to do that will be covered in subsequent chapters of this section of the book.

But in this chapter, we will look in greater depth as to why God made us in order to demonstrate His goodness. My personal answer to that 3rd question of the Baltimore Catechism noted above would also include to demonstrate His great love.

We are provided some insights as to why He created us in the first book of the Bible, Genesis. When God created human beings, He said: *Let us make man in our image, after our likeness. Let them have dominion over the fish of the sea, the birds of the air, and the cattle, and over all the wild animals and all the creatures that crawl on the ground. God created man in his image, in the divine image he created them; male and female he created them.*

The above words of God do not tell us exactly why He decided to make humans, but rather He gave us the words from which we can better understand. Our Heavenly Father is the Creator and Master of all things. He has Dominion over all his creation, but He indicated by his words, His willingness to share that dominion with his human creation.

His willingness to share in his Dominion contains much of the answer to how we are made in his image and likeness. His first sentence noted above states that He wished to make humans in His image and after his likeness. He immediately followed those words with giving humans dominion over his other animal creations. Genesis then goes on to state that not only were humans created in his image but in his "divine image".

When God the Father sent his Son to earth, the Son reminded us several times that the greatest commandment was for us to love God with all our heart, soul, mind, and strength. That was our heavenly Father's expectation from his human creation. When the Father created humans, he did not create robotic humans but rather he gave them a free will. It was in using that free will that He expected the reciprocation of His great love for those humans he wished to one day be members of his Heavenly Kingdom.

But his first human creations, Adam and Eve, disobeyed the only commandment our Heavenly Father gave them and thus sin entered the world. But that did not terminate the Father's love for his earthly children. Time after time our Heavenly Father has forgiven his wayward children.

The Heavenly Father's love for his human creation is a divine and perfect love. It does not cease because his earthly human creations stray. In his perfect wisdom He foresaw that his earthly children would stray, but that did not preclude His creation of them so they might one day share in his Heavenly Kingdom. The Biblical story of the Prodigal Son is the story of our Heavenly Father's great love for us despite our sinful faults.

God would not only forgive us; He would send His only begotten Son to suffer and die on the Cross for our sins. There is no greater demonstration of God's love, than the death on the Cross which was endured to expiate our sins and to open the gates of his Kingdom for us.

The creation of humans in his divine image included the spiritual soul. During his time on earth Jesus told us that our flesh (body) was of no avail but that our spirit (soul) gives us life. It is through our soul that we repent of our sins and thereby seek again and again the love of our Heavenly Father as did the Prodigal Son. It is only in God that humans find the truth and happiness for which they search. When humans seek happiness only from the things of earth, they fail to find true happiness.

Very early in Part One, the Catechism of the Catholic Church explains in CCC 27 how humans find such happiness:

The desire for God is written in the human heart, because man is created by God and for God; and God never ceases to draw man to himself. Only in God will he find the truth and happiness he never stops searching for:

The dignity of man rests above all on the fact that he is called to communion with God. This invitation to converse with God is addressed to man as soon as he comes into being. For if man exists, it is because God has created him through love, and through love continues to hold him in existence. He cannot live fully according to truth unless he freely acknowledges that love and entrusts himself to his creator.

No matter how much we try to explain in human terms, the great and divine love God has for his created humans, we will always fall short. It cannot be explained in human terms because the language of flawed humans cannot capture or explain the magnitude of our heavenly Father's divine love and goodness. Our heavenly Father understands our inability to love as He loves us, but he expects us to do our best to love Him with all our heart, soul, mind and strength.

CHAPTER 2

THE TOILS OF HUMANS

"My yoke is easy and my burden is light". These words of our Lord told us that we would have toils on earth, but they were endurable if we put our faith in Him.

Our Lord used the above words partially to rebuke the numerous rules and procedures with which the Pharisees burdened the Jewish people. Our Lord supported those rules and procedures but also made it clear that love of Him and neighbor were superior to the blind observance of those rules.

It is a tendency of nations and religions to impose many rules and procedures on those they govern. The danger of doing that is no different at the present time than it was at the time of our Lord. They often lay heavy burdens on those living under such rules and procedures.

In comparison to the rules and procedures placed on humans by both secular and religious governments, the rules of our Lord are easy and light because they are based on love of God and love of neighbor. Love makes all things easier and the greater the love the easier and lighter are the yoke and burden. If his commands to love were carried out perfectly we would indeed have heaven on earth.

Our toils on earth encompass both secular and spiritual burdens. In order to earn a living on earth, most of us must endure work in the secular section of society. It is fair to ask how we can observe our Lord's commands while we spend much of our day working.

When we look upon our daily toils as a sacrifice to our Lord and recall the greatest of all sacrifices, we can turn those toils into joy. His great sacrifice for us was his passion and death on the cross for our sins. Few of us are rarely asked to suffer for Him as He suffered for us. But we can recall his sacrifice for us as we go through our daily chores.

Some of us, such as farmers, do our daily toils in a solitary manner. That type of work permits us time for daily prayers and to focus on the beauty of God's creations. We can spend many hours of our day in that way.

Most of us have jobs that involve other people. In such work we have the opportunity to remember our Lord's words to love our neighbor as our self and to love one another as He loved us. We have many opportunities to use the words "please" and "thank you" when working with others. Doing that can turn our work into joy.

It is not only in the secular world that human toil

takes place. Increasing our faith also involves struggles. We cannot serve both God and mammon at the same time so increasing our faith requires greater focus on the things of God and less focus on the things of the world. It is our purpose in this world to better know, love and serve Him. To do that requires a greater commitment of our time and a great focus on our prayers.

It is unfortunate that far too many people of our world, and especially in the United States, have become more focused on the things of the world than the things of God. The results of that have become ever more obvious as hatred and divisiveness all too frequently replace love of God and neighbor. When things of the world replace love of God and neighbor, the lust for worldly power becomes more pervasive.

In order to give God the amount of time in our daily lives which He deserves, we must be willing to sacrifice and to be disciplined in setting aside time for our Creator.

It is easy for humans to ignore their Creator as they go about performing their daily toils. For that reason, it is important to establish prayer and other worship times during the day. The greater our focus on our Savior, the greater our joy will be on earth. It will also help us in our goal of eternal happiness with Him.

In recent years, our Church has placed less emphasis on sacrifice and piety. That is unfortunate, because those virtues are important to demonstrate love of our Lord and neighbor. When we sacrifice our own desires for God and neighbor, we demonstrate our love for them. Too often these days we look first to satisfying our own desires. That becomes a practice in selfishness and leads to the aforementioned hatred and divisiveness. Our Church would be well-served to again remind all parishioners of the sacredness involved in sacrifice and piety. It also helps remind us of the love our Lord demonstrated for us during his time on earth.

Yes, he reminded us that his yoke is easy and his burden is light. If we understand that, what we call toils can be used to demonstrate our love of Him and our neighbors. We can turn those toils into joy. By accepting our toils as a sacrifice for our Lord, we also better emulate Him. He sacrificed Himself for love of us. We are greater lovers of his first great commandment if we do the same for Him.

CHAPTER 3

KNOW HIM

In order to better love and serve our Lord, we must know Him better. In Matthew 16, Jesus addressed this question to his disciples; "But who do you say that I am?" *Simon Peter said in reply, "You are the Messiah, the Son of the living God." Jesus said to him in reply, "Blessed are you Simon, son of Jonah. For flesh and blood has not revealed this to you but my heavenly Father."*

That question to Peter, followed by Peter's answer identified for us the greatest and only divine and human person, who has walked upon this earth. But that question is addressed to each of us as well. During our life on earth, our most important quest is to answer our Lord's question beyond that given by Peter.

Our Lord and Savior came to earth to die upon the Cross to redeem our sins. But during his time on earth, he also taught us what we must do to one day be with Him through all eternity.

To all of us on earth He was our Spiritual Teacher. Through his direct commands, teachings and parables,

He gave us the information we need to know, in order to fulfill our purpose on earth.

Faith is a very individualistic, spiritual attribute of the human soul. We grow that faith when we better understand the majesty and love of our Divine Savior. The greatest way for me personally to better know Him is to dwell on the two great commandments He gave us in the 22nd Chapter of Matthew:

"You shall love the Lord, your God, with all your heart, with all your soul, and with all your mind. This is the greatest and the first commandment. The second is like it: You shall love your neighbor as yourself. The whole law and the prophets depend on these two commandments."

If the whole law and the prophets depend on these two commandments, then it seems incumbent on us to understand as best we can those two commandments. Our Lord spent his three years in public life teaching us how to best understand his two greatest commandments. What He taught us is set forth in the Sacred Scriptures, which are inspired by the Holy Spirit. Therefore, to better know and understand our Lord requires us to better know, understand and love the teachings He gave us that are contained in the Bible.

It is a good practice to set aside some time each day to read Sacred Scripture and to try to better understand and put into action what our Lord taught us. In our flawed humanity, we will never fully understand or practice all He taught us, but by dwelling on that which He taught us we can better understand.

In order to better understand, we must believe that

everything contained in the Bible has been inspired by the Holy Spirit and to better understand what Our Lord taught us means that we must first believe that the Bible gives us "TRUTH". It is not our chore to try to interpret His words in a way that we would like but rather in a way that He wants us to believe. Only then can we better understand TRUTH. To believe helps us to better understand.

How then can we better believe and better understand? We need to receive His grace and blessings to do that. We need to pray for those graces and blessings.

One way for people in the Catholic religion to better understand is to attend Daily Mass. Over the course of several years the daily readings from Sacred Scripture will cover most of the Bible. We also have the homily by a priest to help us understand those readings. Other Christian religions also include the readings of Sacred Scripture at their services.

For those who cannot attend Daily Mass, it is a good practice as noted earlier, to set aside some time each day to read Sacred Scriptures.

In order to better understand Truth, we need spiritual wisdom. In my opinion the growth of faith and growth in spiritual wisdom are closely related. To better know our Lord, we need to grow in both faith and spiritual wisdom.

In Chapter 9 verse 10 of Proverbs, we are told the following: *The beginning of wisdom is the fear of the Lord, and knowledge of the Holy One is understanding.* It can be difficult to believe that we must fear the Lord in order to have spiritual growth.

The word fear can have several meanings as used in Proverbs. Fear can be defined as apprehension when one is facing danger. Fear can also indicate great respect. It can also include great reverence and respect. We can probably state that "fear of the Lord" is an amalgamation of all those definitions and maybe more.

We should stand in fear of the Holy One who will be our Judge and who knows and evaluates our every thought, word and deed. We should also have a great respect for the One who is the Creator and Master of all that exists. Great reverence and respect are due to One who can be as majestic and loving as our God. We err in our understanding of the Holy One when we do not fear Him as suggested in Proverbs.

If we are to know Him better, we must have that fear in order to move onward and upward to greater understanding, greater faith and greater wisdom. It is vital to our human soul that we appreciate the words of Proverbs. To grow in faith, and to better understand and know the Holy One, it is a necessity that we accept and search for correct belief. It is through faith and correct belief that we can grow in our knowledge of Him, who created us.

As Christians and Catholics, we have numerous ways to help us better know and understand He who made us. We have Sacred Scripture, which is the most common way for all Christians to better know Him. For those of us who are Catholics, we also have the

Catechism, Magisterium, along with writings of the hierarchy, doctors of the Church, saints and theological scholars of the Church to assist us in better knowing Him. As previously noted, attendance at Daily Mass is another way to better know Him.

But in addition to the methods just noted in the prior paragraph, we can also get to know Him by being closer to Him in our daily lives. All of us can spend time in prayer. As Catholics we can also be closer to Him through the reception of Holy Communion, whereby we join our human nature with his Divine nature. Receiving Holy Communion was his special request to "Do This in Memory of Me". One of my personal best ways to try to know Him better is by attendance at the Exposition of the Blessed Sacrament. It is a wonderful and blessed way to spend time where we are simply thankful for his great love for us and his majesty.

Knowing Him better is a prerequisite to better loving and serving Him.

CHAPTER 4

LOVE HIM

How do we love Him whom we cannot see? In this life we believe love to be an emotional, affectionate and sentimental tie to someone we hold dear to us. Our love of God must be that and more since we cannot see or be physically with Him. Our love of God must transcend that earthly love of others. He must be the center of our life. We must recognize Him as One who is the Creator and Master of all things, both visible and invisible, including ourselves. He is the one who so loved us that He suffered and died for us. He is the one who taught us how we must live and sent the Holy Spirit to show us the right path.

In his encyclical on Love of God, Pope Benedict XVI, wrote of what our love of God entails:

The love-story between God and man consists in the very fact that this communion of will increases in a communion of thought and sentiment, and thus our will and God's will increasingly coincide: God's will is no longer for me an alien will, something imposed on me from without by the commandments, but it is now my own will, based on the realization that God is in fact more deeply present to me than I am to myself. The abandonment to God increases and God becomes our joy.

The best way for me to experience that "communion of will" is through the reception of the Holy Eucharist at the celebration of the Mass. It is truly a time when we are in a Holy Communion with the presence of our Savior. It is a time when we receive Him who suffered and died on the cross for us so one day we might be able to spend eternity with Him. There is no greater sacrament, by which we align ourselves with Him to the degree we do in Holy Communion. It is truly the apex of our Catholic faith. In the reception of the Holy Eucharist, we also fulfill the invitation He made to all of us at the Last Supper. "Do This in Memory of Me".

All Christians have the ability to love our God through prayers of thanksgiving and intercessions. Praying often to demonstrate our Love of Him who died for us is an expectation He has from us, and it should be a way to help us grow toward the "communion of will", of which Pope Benedict spoke.

At his Last Supper Discourse, Jesus told his Apostles of another way to show our love of Him. "If you love me you will keep my commandments". By keeping his commandments, we demonstrate to Him that we live as He wants us to live. In his Last Supper Discourse our Lord made additional comments on the importance of love. In Chapter 14: 21 he stated, "Whoever has my commandments and observes them is the one who loves me. And whoever loves me will be loved by my Father, and I will love him and reveal myself to him."

His Last Supper Discourse given on that night before He died for us, gave us several comments on the importance of love. In Chapter 15 of John, he went on to state; "This is my commandment: love one another as I love you. No one has greater love than this, to lay down one's life for one's friends."

The commandment He gave us to love one another as He loves us is a very high standard. None of us will be able to reach the heights of that bar during our life on earth, but He expects us to try.

Humility and obedience are important virtues in demonstrating our love of our God. Humility is of importance because we constantly need to remind ourselves that doing his will throughout our day is of greater importance than following our desires of earthly temptations. Obedience is also of great importance, because it is a necessity to accepting all He taught us during his time on earth.

Humility is also important in understanding that God must be the center of our life. It is through understanding that we accept what it means to love Him with all our heart, soul, mind and strength. To continuously move closer to a more perfect communion of wills requires us to accept that his will is always the perfect will.

Earlier in this chapter, I noted that it was through the reception of the Holy Eucharist, that I feel most aligned with He who created us. It is a time when our human body is joined with He who is both human and divine.

Another important time to spend with our Lord is during the Adoration of the Blessed Sacrament. It is a time when our purpose is to adore and glorify our Lord. It is a wonderful time to thank Him for all the graces and blessings He has bestowed on us. It helps us to increase our love of him.

As Christians we all have our individual faith in our Lord. The common thread for all is to be joined with our Creator in a communion of wills. We are all sinners and must concede that our flawed way is not the only way of expressing and demonstrating love of our God. But it is our purpose on earth to pursue our love of Him in the manner we choose.

As Christians and as Catholics we can also demonstrate our love of God by not only accepting his commands but by learning to love his commands. Sacred Scriptures are composed not just of words but by words that are inspired by the Holy Spirit. To better learn how to live our lives on earth, a better discernment of love of his written word is a substantial help as we pray; "Thy will be done on earth as it is in Heaven". By accepting and loving his commands and directions given in Sacred Scriptures, we also fulfill that for which we pray.

We also have Apostolic Tradition to help us love our Creator. By accepting and loving that which our Church teaches regarding faith and morals, we make it easier to love our Lord. Debating instead of accepting, does not aid us on our journey to eternal life.

We end this chapter with words from the Prologue in the Catechism of the Catholic Church. "The whole concern of doctrine and its teaching must be directed to the love that never ends". To that we say Amen.

CHAPTER 5

SERVE HIM

As our faith grows and as we better know Him and love Him, we will want to serve Him who made us. Our Lord himself told us in John 14:12 that "whoever believes in me will do the works that I do". In doing the works He did, we serve our Lord.

On the day this chapter was first being drafted, the Gospel reading provided us with a great insight on how Jesus himself prioritized the way to love and serve Him. The reading was from the 10th Chapter of Luke:

As they continued their journey he entered a village where a woman whose name was Martha welcomed him. She had a sister named Mary who sat beside the Lord at his feet listening to him speak. Martha, burdened with much serving came to him and said, "Lord, do you not care that my sister has left me by myself to do the serving? Tell her to help me." The Lord said to her in reply, "Martha, Martha, you are anxious and worried about many things. There is need of only one thing. Mary has chosen the better part and it will not be taken from her."

While Martha was doing good works in preparing food for our Lord, He makes it clear that loving, listening and serving Him is a higher priority.

Our Lord's first and greatest commandment is to love Him with all our heart, soul, mind and strength. In obedience to that commandment, we also indicate our love of Him while also serving Him. Our religion can be a significant vehicle in helping us love and serve Him.

As a member of the Catholic faith and religion, I am provided with a number of ways to love and serve Him. Frequent attendance at Mass, including reception of the Holy Eucharist rank high, if not highest, on the ways we can love and serve Him. It has been a long-held belief of mine that we cannot love and serve our Lord better than through the reception of Holy Communion, where we link our human nature to his divine and human nature. As noted in the prior chapter, through the reception of the Holy Eucharist, we also answer his invitation to "Do This in Memory of Me."

Another way to love and serve our Lord is through attendance at the Exposition of the Blessed Sacrament. It is a special, quiet time when we can dedicate an hour or as long as we wish to thank our Lord for all the blessings and graces He has bestowed on us.

All of us have the opportunity to better love and serve him through our prayers. Communicating with our Lord during the course of the day is always a good way to demonstrate our love and service to Him.

Finding reminders to help us pray during the day is useful. When we first arise in the morning it is good to begin our day with morning prayers. Before and after meals is another good time to pray. Evening prayers, including an Examen of the day, is always a good way to end our day.

Many of us, also have favorite places to pray. Our Church as well as our home probably are at the head of that list. As a young man, I spent several years in a Franciscan seminary in Westmont, Illinois. That property included a replica of the Porziuncola Chapel built by St. Francis and his fellow Franciscans in Assisi. On my walks around the property, I rarely missed entering the chapel for some prayer time. Many of us no doubt have similar places where we like to pray.

Prayer is a practice of almost all religions. That is also a good reason to respect all religions.

At the beginning of this chapter, we noted that our Lord told us that if we have faith in Him, we will do the works He did. That is why we have used the beginning of this chapter to state ways we can grow our faith. It is a logical extension of his words, that if we grow our faith, we will also grow in ways we can do the works He did.

During his time on earth our Lord did much to help the poor and disabled. He was compassionate to lepers and others who live in the margin of society. It is important for us to do the same. When we have faith in Him, and love our neighbors as our self, it is a fair question to ask what that should involve.

Humans should not be over-enamored with things of earth, but humans should properly expect a life that provides them the basic needs of food and shelter. That human need should be a consideration when we decide how we can love our neighbor. Through the goodness of the Lord, many of us are blessed with treasures and all of us are blessed with time and talent. These blessings should be used in a manner that makes us good stewards of what has been given to us.

If we love our neighbors as ourselves, we should want for them what we want for ourselves, in the way of basic human needs. In addition to the necessities of life, that desire for others includes love. All of us wish to be loved.

In the world we live in today, there are many ways we can help our neighbor. Many charitable organizations exist which are established to help others. We can help such organizations by supporting them with our treasures, time and talent. In doing that we should not overlook our Church, because as we wish for a blessed eternal life, we should also wish that for our neighbor. The spiritual needs of our neighbors are as important or more important than their earthly needs.

When we serve others, we serve our Lord. He said, "What you do to the least of my brethren you do unto me."

DEATH

CHAPTER 6

THE SEPARATION OF THE BODY AND SOUL

Some years ago, I attended the 50th wedding anniversary of a couple with whom we had been friends for many years. As we somewhat jokingly discussed our advancing age my friend noted that death was not a great fear, but the process of dying was.

But the prospect of death is and should be of concern to us and how prepared we are to face our Lord and how prepared we are for eternal life. That concern is a proper reason that the Book of Proverbs in the Old Testament tells us that fear of the Lord is the beginning of wisdom.

Fear of the Lord is the beginning of wisdom and as we move through life, that fear can help us grow in our faith, which in turn helps prepare us for the day when our body and soul separate until they will again be joined together at the resurrection of our body. To some degree, we will remain in doubt about our life after death, because we are sinners and although we believe in his forgiveness, none of us know for sure how prepared we are for Heaven.

In preparing our body and soul for eternity, it is good to reflect on words spoken and written by Saint Oscar Romero, who was the Archbishop of El Salvador at the time he was murdered at the altar:

A preaching that does not point out sin is not the preaching of the gospel. A preaching that makes sinners feel good, so that they become entrenched in their sinful state, betrays the gospel's call....

A preaching that awakens, a preaching that enlightens—as when a light turned on awakens, and of course annoys a sleeper --that is the preaching of Christ, calling:

Wake up! Be converted!

That is the church's authentic preaching.

To those good St. Romero's words, I can only say, Amen.

In a Church that today draws poor attendance and where many do not believe in the Real Prescence of the Holy Eucharist, we can only wonder if that is a Church that is somehow betraying the gospel's call. In preparing the human body for death and the soul for judgment, it does not portray the breadth and depth of the preaching of Christ to focus only on preaching that makes sinners feel good and makes sin appear acceptable.

The words of St. Romero should be a reminder of what our Lord told us in Chapter 7:13&14 of the gospel of Matthew: *Enter through the narrow gate; for the gate is wide and the road broad that leads to destruction, and those who enter through it are many. How narrow the gate and constricted the road that leads to life. And those who find it are few.*

When we preach and ignore those words of our Lord, we indeed betray the gospel's call for repentance.

It is good for teachers, preachers and writers to frequently remind us of the great love of our Lord. But it is also important and wise to remind us that we will be judged by a just God.

As we prepare for the departure of the soul from our deceased body, we should constantly remind ourselves that sin stains our soul and that repentance and resolution against further sinning is part of such preparation.

As noted earlier, our Lord reminded us that the gate is narrow, and the road constricted which leads to eternal life with Him. He also said that only a few find it. So how do we find that narrow road? It is not an easy answer but if I would try to describe it briefly, I would say it is a road that relates solely to the things of God.

Even when we understand the things of God, our flawed body tends to stray from that road. Life is a perpetual struggle to stay on that road and to return to it when we stray from it.

It is difficult but possible to make God the center of our life throughout most of each day. Yes, students are in the classroom much of the day and many of us are at our workplace. But, as St. Therese, the Little Flower, taught us, when we live as God wishes us to live, we can do so even when we are in the classroom or at work. When we interact with others, we can do that as God wishes us to do it. Throughout the day, we can indicate that we do love our neighbor as our self.

As noted several times in this chapter, we will at times stray from the path. But we can repent those times we stray and sin and make a firm purpose of amendment to do better in the future. Every day of our lives will be open on that judgment day when our soul departs from our body. A loving God will be a forgiving God, but He will also be a just God, and for that reason we should fear Him and grow in wisdom.

All of us will face death and upon our death we will be judged immediately and will be rewarded or condemned in accordance with our works on earth and on our faith in Him. We refer to that judgment as the Particular Judgment. We believe that if we are found worthy, we will enter into the blessedness of heaven immediately or may require the purification of Purgatory before such entrance occurs. Those found not worthy will be condemned to everlasting damnation in Hell.

Our Church teaches that to be found worthy and enter Heaven is "to be with Christ". There, they live the perfect life with the Holy Trinity, the Blessed Mother and with the angels and other saints. The Church goes on to tell us that our union with those just noted will be "fulfillment of the deepest human longings, the state of supreme, definitive happiness".

The soul will remain in Heaven until joined with the resurrected and glorified body at our Savior's second coming.

CHAPTER 7

THE JOURNEY OF THE SOUL

There is much about our human soul that is a mystery. But Sacred Scripture and Church teaching leave no doubt that all humans are endowed with a soul by our Creator.

The Catechism of the Catholic Church in paragraph 366 tells us about the creation of the human soul as follows:

The Church teaches that every spiritual soul is created immediately by God – it is not "produced" by the parents – and also that it is immortal: it does not perish when it separates from the body at death, and it will be reunited with the body at the final Resurrection.

The Church also teaches that the body and soul are not two separate natures but rather they form a single nature. How the body and soul interact is also subject to much mystery. Because of the mystery, we will rely substantially on Sacred Scripture and Church teaching to further define the important role our soul plays. Some years ago, I published a book "The Wisdom of our Soul". We will also rely to some degree on the research done for that book.

It is important for everyone to understand that the soul is a direct creation of God. We should also remember that all of God's creations are great. It is when the decisions of the flawed human body override the promptings of our soul (conscience) that we sin. It is a struggle for human beings to let the soul dominate our words and deeds.

In a letter to the Galatians, St. Paul made very stark contrasts between the body (flesh) and the soul (Spirit):

I say, then: live by the Spirit and you will certainly not gratify the desire of the flesh. For the flesh has desires against the Spirit and the Spirit against the flesh; these are opposed to each other, so that you may not do what you want. But if you are guided by the Spirit, you are not under the law. Now the works of the flesh are obvious; immorality, impurity, licentiousness, idolatry, sorcery, hatreds, rivalry, jealousy, outbursts of fury, acts of selfishness, dissensions, factions, occasions of envy, drinking bouts, orgies, and the like. I warn you as I warned you before, that those who do such things will not inherit the kingdom of God.

In contrast, the fruit of the Spirit is love, joy, peace, patience, kindness, generosity, faithfulness, gentleness, self-control. Against these there is no law. Now those who belong to Christ have crucified their flesh with its passions and desires. If we live in the Spirit, let us also follow the Spirit. Let us not be conceited, provoking one another, envious of one another.

St. Paul could not have been clearer on the path we must follow to "inherit the kingdom of God". We need to follow the promptings of our soul. In following the promptings of our soul, we fulfill our purpose in life to know, love and serve Him. It is the soul that is the "spiritual principle" in humans and is "of greatest value" to them.

From the earliest years of humans, the struggle to follow the promptings of the soul has been a lifetime struggle. When we fail in that struggle, it is of great importance for us to repent and seek God's forgiveness and mercy. Our compassionate God understands that we are flawed and will sometimes sin.

During our time on earth, it is the soul who is our conscience. The soul reminds us of the path we should follow during our time on earth, but our flesh all too often pulls us from that spiritual path. It is the soul that reminds us of the need for repentance and amendment.

There is much about the soul that is a mystery. Earlier in this chapter we noted the many good virtues that St. Paul listed about the soul. Given those virtues it might seem that all souls created by God would be destined for Heaven. But that is not necessarily the case.

In chapter 13 of Luke, our Lord gave us a parable to better help us understand how our soul can be led astray. *There once was a person who had a fig tree planted in his orchard, and when he came in search of fruit on it but found none, he said to the gardener, "For three years now I have come in search of fruit on this fig tree but have found none. So cut it down. Why should it exhaust the soil?" He said to him in reply, "Sir, leave if for this year also, and I shall cultivate the ground around it and fertilize it; it may bear fruit in the future. If not you can cut it down."*

And so it is with our soul. If we succumb to the sinfulness of the flesh and do not repent, we eventually permit our soul to wither and cease bearing fruit. The journey of our soul toward the path to eternal salvation and bliss is a lifelong struggle against the sinful traits of the body as described by St. Paul.

As noted at the beginning of this chapter there is much about our soul that is a mystery. But the Church and Sacred Scripture do give us insight to the great value our soul has to us during our life on earth. Of even greater mystery is the life of the soul following the body's death and prior to the resurrection of the body.

Not much information of the life of the soul following the death of the body is available in either Sacred Scripture or Church teaching.

However, during the Crucifixion of our Lord, he spoke words to the good thief that provide some insight. Chapter 24 of Luke's gospel states the following: *Now one of the criminals hanging there reviled Jesus, saying, "Are you not the Messiah? Save yourself and us." The other, however, rebuking him, said in reply, "Have you no fear of God, for you are subject to the same condemnation? And indeed, we have been condemned justly, for the sentence we received corresponds to our crimes, but this man has done nothing criminal." Then he said, "Jesus remember me when you come into your kingdom." He replied to him, "Amen, I say to you today you will be with me in Paradise."*

We know that Jesus had to be speaking of the good thief's soul because his body would die that day. We also know that Jesus promised the good thief that his soul would be with Him in Paradise (Heaven or possibly

Purgatory) on that very same day. We can further deduce that the good thief's soul would immediately or eventually experience a blissful life with our Lord in Heaven, as will all other souls in Heaven.

But what that blissful life entails for any specific soul is left in the category of mystery. Whether or not, the soul has a similar power of reasoning as it did when united with the body before death also remains in the mysterious category. We do believe that the soul will be subject to the Lord's Particular Judgment upon death of the body, but how that Judgment will be understood by the soul also remains a mystery. Will the souls destined for Purgatory receive information on what purification is still required?

CHAPTER 8

THE REUNIFICATION OF THE BODY AND SOUL

A s Christians and Catholics, we express our belief in the resurrection of the body when we recite the Apostles Creed. Our faith which stems from his Resurrection gives us the hope that our own resurrection will result in spending eternity in the company of He who died for us.

The resurrection of the body has been a basic belief of our Christian faith from the beginning. In his letter to the Corinthians St. Paul made that very clear. *But if Christ is preached as raised from the dead, how can some among you say that there is no resurrection of the dead? If there is no resurrection of the dead, then neither has Christ been raised. And if Christ has not been raised, then empty too is our preaching: empty too your faith. Then we are also false witnesses to God, because we testified against God that he raised Christ, whom he did not raise if in fact the dead are not raised.*

That is about as straightforward as any words given

us by St. Paul. Our Christian faith is tied to our Lord's Resurrection, which in turn provides us the belief for our own resurrection.

In the 5th Chapter of John's gospel, we are also assured of the resurrection of the body: *Amen, amen, I say to you, the hour is coming and is now here when the dead will hear the voice of the Son of God, and who hear will live. For just as the Father has life in himself, so also he gave to his Son the possession of life in himself. And he gave him power to exercise judgment, because he is the Son of Man. Do not be amazed at this, because the hour is coming in which all who are in the tombs will hear his voice and will come out, those who have done good deeds to the resurrection of life, but those who have done wicked deeds to the resurrection of condemnation.*

Our Church tells us that our body decays after death while our soul goes to meet God and awaits the reunion with its glorified body. Through the power of our Lord's resurrection our bodies will be granted incorruptibility as they are reunited with our souls. All the dead will rise.

How this reunion of our body and soul will take place is beyond our human understanding and it is a matter of faith that we believe it will take place. Sacred Scripture tells us that this reunification will take place "at the last day".

This glorious resurrection of our body together with the reunification with our soul should provide us a never-ending reminder of the merits of living our life as God would have us live it. But we are flawed humans. Nevertheless, we are also assured that we can be with our Lord one day, if when we fail, we repent and seek his forgiveness. It was because of those failures that He died on the Cross for us.

During his time on earth, our Lord reminded us numerous times to be prepared for the day we would depart from this earth. "Stay awake" were his words to remind us that our time on earth is a preparation for our time in eternity. Each morning when we awaken, we need to remind ourselves to live the day as God would have us live it. Not only does such living better prepare us for our future life with Him, but it would also help fulfil the words of our Lord's Prayer; "Thy Kingdom come, thy will be done on earth as it is in Heaven".

In living such a life, we are better prepared for that day when our body will be reunited with our soul. In living each and every day in accordance with his will, our body and soul will also be best prepared for "the last day".

St. Augustine gave us words to help remind us of the importance of dying with Christ. *It is better for me to die in Christ Jesus than to reign over the ends of the earth. Him it is I seek – who died for us. I am on the point of giving birth…. Let me receive pure light; when I shall have arrived there, then shall I be a man.*

Christian death is merely the end of humans' earthly pilgrimage and journey, which prepares us for our eternal life in accord with our Savior's divine plan.

The Resurrection of the Lord may provide some insight to our own resurrection. Following his Resurrection, He was not recognized by Mary Magdalene, who had been close to Him before the Resurrection. He was also not recognized by others who were close to Him. How our own glorified body may be changed on that last day is unknown.

The Holy Eucharist also provides us a "foretaste of Christ's transfiguration of our bodies" from words provided us by St. Irenaeus:

Just as bread that comes from the earth, after God's blessing has been invoked upon it, is no longer ordinary bread, but Eucharist, formed of two things, the one earthly and the other heavenly: so too our bodies, which partake of the Eucharist, are no longer corruptible, but possess the hope of resurrection. The Eucharist is truly a linking of the human with the divine.

As noted earlier, there is much regarding the reunification of the glorified body and soul that is beyond human understanding. But through faith we understand that it will happen and for the righteous it will be an eternity of living with Him who wrought our salvation. We can only meditate in thanksgiving on what that eternal life will be like in a "new heaven and a new earth".

We close this chapter with a reminder from "The Imitation of Christ" on how to live our life on earth so we are prepared for that eternal life.

Every action of yours, every thought, should be those of one who expects to die before the day is out. Death would have no great terrors for you if you had a quiet conscience…. Then why not keep clear of sin instead of running away from death? If you are not fit to face death today, it's very unlikely you will be tomorrow….

JUDGMENT

CHAPTER 9

THE PARTICULAR JUDGMENT

Upon the death of our body, our soul will immediately face the Particular Judgment. That is a belief of the Catholic Church which includes the belief that the soul will then be sent to Heaven, Purgatory or Hell. The inclusion of Purgatory as an option for the soul is not a belief of many Protestant religions.

Very little reference is made in either Sacred Scripture or in Church teaching, to the life of the soul following the period after the death of the body and before the Final Judgment on the last day. That period in the life of the soul is a period of mystery.

We, as Catholics believe in the Particular Judgment based in large part from our Lord's parable regarding the poor man Lazarus and also on the words our Lord spoke to the good thief on the day of their Crucifixions. Reference to the latter has previously been made in this book. There is no disputing that our Lord promised that the good thief would be with Him in Paradise "this day". We do not know with certainty if that reference to Paradise was a reference to Heaven or to Purgatory.

As Catholics, we also believe that the Particular Judgment is specific to each soul (hence the word Particular). We believe that Judgment results in the soul being destined to Heaven, Purgatory or Hell.

The belief in a Purgatory accepts that souls going there die in God's grace and friendship but need additional purification in order that their soul will rise to the level of holiness needed to enter Heaven.

It is a reasonable question for people of faith to wonder what the purification experience will be during the soul's time spent in Purgatory. Some of our Saints have had experiences that have enabled them to express their views. Included in such saints are St. Catherine of Genoa, St. Faustina, Padre Pio and several others.

The common thread of the views of the saints seems to be that Purgatory consists of great pain and great joy. The great pain is the result of not being with God while the great joy comes from the knowledge that one day they will be with God.

It is also an understanding of the saints that the souls in Purgatory long for those of us on earth to pray for them and an especially important way of prayer is through attendance at Mass and having Masses said on behalf of the souls in Purgatory.

Even with what the saints tell us, there is much about the experience of the souls in Purgatory that is impossible for humans to understand.

We will spend much of the remainder of this

chapter addressing some of those mysterious issues. If the greatest suffering of the souls in purgatory is the separation from God, it is a good question to ponder why that same suffering does not affect our souls during our time on earth. We can ponder that question during our time on earth. Will our soul upon death experience an enlightenment that elevates the love of God and thus makes the separation from Him more painful? Is our body so enamored with earthly mammon that it suppresses the soul's longing for God? These and other similar questions can be made a part of our daily Examen to help us elevate love of God and our neighbor.

The love of neighbor should not be overlooked. When we love one another as God loves us, we can become more conscious of the importance of loving our neighbor. We will never be too kind.

Another mysterious issue relates to the time that we may have to spend in purgatory to purify our souls to the level that merits entry into Heaven. Is it time or is it the degree of purification necessary to arrive at the level of love of God and neighbor that will determine the soul's length of stay in Purgatory?

It is the belief of many that Purgatory will no longer be a destination for the soul once the day of Final Judgment arrives. That leads to a question of how the souls living at the time or shortly prior to the time of Final Judgment will be able to be purified, assuming such purification is required.

One of the assuring comments we have from our Sacred Scripture regarding our entry into Heaven or

Purgatory is found in St. Paul's letter to the Romans: *for, if you confess with your mouth that Jesus is Lord and believe in your heart that God raised him from the dead you will be saved. For one believes with the heart and so is justified, and one confesses with the mouth and so is saved. For the scripture says, "No one who believes in him will be put to shame."*

The anticipation of our Particular Judgment should, to some degree, cause us some of the same pain or anxiety and joy that the souls in Purgatory experience. We should be concerned every day that we do not deserve immediate entry into Heaven due to our lack of love, but we should also be joyful for those times we love our Lord with all our heart, soul, mind and strength and our neighbor as our self.

That anticipation should also make us appreciate the words from the Book of Proverbs that fear of the Lord is the beginning of wisdom. That fear should cultivate spiritual wisdom because we must understand that our entry into Heaven is dependent on how great our love is of the Lord. His love is perfect, and we need to elevate our love of Him and neighbor to a level that we can never be sure we have reached. That fear should in turn motivate the elevation of love we need to spend eternity with Him in Heaven.

If we do not fear the Lord and do not fear the day of our Particular Judgment, we lack wisdom.

CHAPTER 10

THE LAST JUDGMENT

Whereas little is contained in Sacred Scripture with specific references to the Particular Judgement, much more is noted regarding the Last Judgment. However, to this writer, some of the references to the Lord's Judgment, are difficult to discern as to whether they are specifically related to the Last Judgment only or may also be references to the Particular Judgment.

This much we can ascertain from the Bible. On the Last Day, for those who have been faithful to our Lord, there will be a wonderful reunion of the glorified body and the soul. We do not know exactly how that reunion will occur in the mind of the glorified body, but we can meditate on what a joyful moment it will be. The knowledge of knowing that together they will spend eternity with our Lord is reason enough to cause an extraordinary happy reunion.

Christians, of many denominations, who may not agree that a Particular Judgment and a Last Judgment will both take place, do generally agree on the words of the Creed which state, "From thence He will come again to judge the living and the dead". That does beg the question of how and where the soul exists prior to the Last Judgment.

The Catholic Church in the Catechism (CCC 675) does state its belief on the trials that will take place prior to the second coming of our Savior:

Before Christ's second coming the Church must pass through a final trial that will shake the faith of many believers. The persecution that accompanies her pilgrimage on earth will unveil the "mystery of iniquity" in the form of a religious deception offering men an apparent solution to their problems at the price of apostasy from the truth. The supreme religious deception is that of the Antichrist, a pseudo-messianism by which man glorifies himself in place of God and of his Messiah come in the flesh.

Those words are difficult to define as to how they will come to take place. Ever since our Lord came to earth there have been those who have offered "men an apparent solution to their problems at the price of apostasy from the truth". In what form the referenced Antichrist will appear and how it is manifested is unknown. And how long such apostasies will last is also unknown.

There have been many views advanced as to Antichrists who have already been on earth as well as views on Antichrists who are yet to come. When so many views and counterviews are expressed, it is often best to look to Church teaching and Sacred Scripture to help readers come to their own conclusions. The view that garners the greatest unanimity is that Antichrists will be a reality.

In the gospels of Matthew and Mark our Lord himself foretold of those who would pretend to be the Messiah. We will use our Lord's words as He gave them (The Great Tribulation) and as provided in the gospel of Matthew 24: 15-28.

"When you see the desolating abomination spoken of through Daniel the prophet standing in the holy place (let the reader understand), then those in Judea must flee to the mountains, a person on the rooftop must not go down to get things out of his house, a person in the field must not return to get his cloak. Woe to pregnant women and nursing mothers in those days. Pray that your flight not be in winter or on the sabbath, for at that time there will great tribulation, such as has not been since the beginning of the world until now or ever will be. And if those days had not been shortened, no one would be saved, but for the sake of the elect they will be shortened. If anyone says to you then, 'Look, there is the Messiah! or, 'There he is!' do not believe it. False messiahs and false prophets will arise, and they will perform signs and wonders so great as to deceive, if that were possible, even the elect. Behold, I have told it to you beforehand. So if they say to you, 'He is in the desert,' do not go out there; if they say, 'He is in the inner rooms,' do not believe it. For just as lightning comes from the east and is seen as far as the west, so will the coming of the Son of Man be. Wherever the corpse is, there the vultures will gather.

Our Lord goes on in Chapter 24 to explain how the Son of Man will return on that last day. In the Last Tribulation discourse above, our Lord does make it clear that antichrists will make claims that are false. Our Lord's words were not long on specifics but are clear as to those who would be with us at those last days.

In the Catechism (CCC 676) our Church goes on to further explain our Lord's words. *The Antichrist's deception already begins to take shape in the world every time the claim is made to realize within history that messianic hope which can only be realized beyond history through the eschatological judgment.* As Our Lord noted in the aforementioned verses from Matthew 24, our Church in CCC 676 goes on to warn us against acceptance of Antichrist assertions that come in other forms, and that includes political forms.

It is my personal view that we have had many forms of such Antichrist assertions since the true Messiah dwelt on earth. There have been such assertions, there are such assertions in the world today and there will continue to be such assertions, most notably as stated by our Lord in Matthew 24. Our time on earth is best spent by loving the true God and thereby loving the commands He gave us. That is our path to the final Promised Land. That is also the best path leading to the group of the righteous we wish to join on the day of the Last Judgment.

None of us know the time or day of the Last Judgment. Each and every day we spend on earth needs to be treated as the last day we may be on earth. On that last day, our Lord and Savior will reveal all the "dispositions of hearts and will render to each man according to his works and according to his acceptance or refusal of grace". When we fully accept the graces and blessings, God bestows on us we will be prepared for that final day.

We conclude this chapter from a teaching of our Church found in CCC 1060 of the Catechism. *At the end of time, the Kingdom of God will come in its fullness. Then the just will reign with Christ forever, glorified in body and soul, and the material universe itself will be transformed. God will then be "all in all" in eternal life.*

After that fullness of time, if we live as He would have us live, we can be in that group of the righteous who will forever enjoy the new Heaven and Earth with He who created all things and sent his only begotten Son to make it possible for us.

ETERNITY

CHAPTER 11

FINAL PURIFICATION

It is a belief of the Catholic Church that souls who are not prepared for Heaven but not condemned to Hell need to undergo a stage of final purification. The Church refers to that stage as Purgatory. We covered some of the aspects of Purgatory in Chapter 9, The Particular Judgment, but we will look at Final Purification from a slightly different viewpoint in this Chapter.

With the exception of the Blessed Virgin Mary, all human creations of God have been sinners. Without the Crucifixion and Resurrection of our Lord and Savior, Heaven would not be available to humans. It was through his suffering, death and Resurrection that Heaven was opened for humans. It is not by our merits that Heaven was opened for those who love Him.

Although, it is not by our efforts that Heaven was made available to us, it is through our efforts that we may one day be found worthy to be with our Lord and Savior in that Kingdom He earned for us.

It is unknown to humans as to that which is required to be found worthy for entrance into Heaven. The Church tells us that those who die in God's grace and friendship <u>and are perfectly purified</u> (underlining added for emphasis), will enter Heaven. But it will be the Judgment of our Lord and Savior to determine which souls are perfectly purified.

It is also a belief of the Church that those who enter Heaven are like God forever. The final purification is therefore a place for those who die in God's grace and friendship but need further purification to enter Heaven.

As noted in the opening paragraph, this chapter was written primarily to view the belief in Purgatory and a Final Purification from a slightly different viewpoint than was covered in Chapter 9. That viewpoint is to view some of the varying beliefs by humans, and different religions.

It is understandable that varying viewpoints exist because little of the Catholic Church's viewpoint can specifically be found in the New Testament. With that lack of underlying evidence, there is much room for different understandings. It is important that we respect the views of others.

In the gospel of John, Chapter 14, Our Lord began his Last Supper Discourse with these words: *"Do not let your hearts be troubled. You have faith in God; have also faith in me. In my Father's house there are many dwelling places. If there were not, would I have told you that I am going to prepare a place for you? And if I go and prepare a place for you, I will come back again and take you to myself, so that where I am going you may also be. Where I am going you know the way.".*

We should not be disheartened that those words leave much room for interpretation. Following the speaking of those words, even his Apostles, Thomas and Philip sought greater clarification. The response of Jesus to the inquisition of Thomas on better trying to understand where Jesus was going was simply that "I am the way and the truth and the life. No one comes to the Father except through me".

That left it to the Apostles and to each of us to determine for ourselves, the importance of living on the path of the way and the truth and the life. How diligently we walk that path determines our place in that "house" of "many dwelling places". It is our spiritual challenge in this life to know Him, love Him and serve him as best we know how in order to be in that house of many places.

The late Pope St. John Paul II spoke of Heaven, Hell and Purgatory as states of being for the soul rather than as places. As humans, who live in a place, it is our tendency to think of them in that manner. It is helpful for all of us to think of our eternal life in the terms described by Pope Saint John Paul II. The Pope's description is very helpful to this writer when thinking of life after death. But after the Final Judgment it is more difficult to assume that there may not be places, because of our belief in a new heaven and earth after the Last Judgment.

The need for final purification also seems logical

to me for other reasons. When I compare my own sin-filled life to that of the late Pope St. John Paul II or Saint Theresa of Calcutta, it is understandable to me that my life has lacked holiness compared with those saints, who seemingly spent their entire life in the service of their Lord.

Sometimes terminology has more to do with what we believe about life after death than does an understanding of the mind. While many Protestant Christians do not believe in "a place" called Purgatory, they do believe the words in Chapter 14 of John. Do they believe that "many dwelling places" include what Catholic Christians describe as Purgatory? I suspect that every Christian living has a slightly different view of life after death.

Purgatory is, in my view, a stage of after-life that will permit me to be purified beyond where my soul may be at the stage of my death. In that regard, it seems to be an opportunity for final purification, which will allow me to be in that place we call Heaven, where we are assured of eternal bliss. In that thought process, it is a stage that we should welcome to ensure that we will eventually be in the company of our Lord, which is the fulfillment of eternal bliss.

If others believe that Heaven is a "house" that has "many dwelling places" and if the possibility exists that such places include what I consider to be a place of final purification, then we are not too far apart in our beliefs.

In the Muslim religion there is a belief that after death there is a place called Araf, which is somewhat akin to Catholics belief in Purgatory. It is important for all of us to be respectful of the religious and spiritual beliefs of others. It is God, who is the keeper of truth. God has revealed as much as He wishes us to believe during our time on earth. He is also the one we refer to as Love. When we love our neighbors and respect their beliefs, we best observe his command to love our neighbor as our self.

It is my belief that many of us on earth who have faith in our Lord, may need additional purification before our entry into Heaven. It is also my belief that we can bypass that step if we dedicate our lives on earth to loving our Lord with all our heart, soul, mind and strength and our neighbor as ourselves. But inasmuch as we are all sinners, we will grow in wisdom if we fear God, because He will be the one who determines how well we lived in accord with his commandments during our time on earth.

CHAPTER 12

HELL – ETERNAL DAMNATION

There are many words that have been spoken and written regarding Hell. There have been many pictures etched and painted regarding Hell. Such words and portrayals vary widely. Therefore, in this chapter, we will make extra efforts to refer to words of Sacred Scripture and Church teachings. We will not find specificity in those words, but we hope they will be helpful to the reader in making their own discernment regarding Hell.

When we speak of Hell and Eternal Damnation it is important to understand that those who go there, after their time on earth is over, do so by their own choice. My personal view of Hell is a place where the souls of those reside, who reject God and love. Because God is love, those who reject love are destined for Hell because of their rejection of love. More on that later.

There should be no illusions that Hell exists. In Matthew 13, Jesus uses several parables to explain its existence. Included in Matthew 13 is the parable of the weeds among the wheat. When his disciples ask Him to do so He explains the parable as follows:

"He who sows good seed is the Son of Man, the field is the world, the good seed the children of the kingdom. The weeds are the children of the evil one, and the enemy who sows them is the devil. The harvest is the end of the age, and the harvesters are angels. Just as weeds are collected and burned up with fire, so will it be at the end of the age. The Son of Man will send his angels, and they will collect out of his kingdom all who cause others to sin and all evildoers. They will throw them into the fiery furnace, where there will be wailing and grinding of teeth. Then the righteous will shine like the sun in the kingdom of their Father. Whoever has ears ought to hear.

It is sad that many who have ears choose not to hear. We are told in the Old Testament that fear of God is the beginning of wisdom. Unfortunately, many also choose to ignore those words. It is a lack of humility and an excess ego that cause some to ignore the love of their Creator and to dismiss Him as the Creator of all things. Hatred and divisiveness are the results of the lack of love. In our world today we can find signs of hell on earth.

It has been said that if atheists truly believe that God does not exist, they should be excused. I find that difficult to believe and contrary to what St. Paul said in his letter to the Romans. The rejection of God and love is a conscious decision of free will and not a choice resulting from a lack of understanding. Let us look at the words of St. Paul's letter to the Romans, Chapter 1 verses 18 to 25:

The wrath of God is indeed being revealed from heaven against every piety and wickedness of those who suppress the truth by their wickedness. For what can be known about God is evident to them because God made it evident to them. Ever since the creation of the world, his invisible attributes of eternal power and divinity have been able to be understood and perceived in what he has made. As a result they have no excuse; for although they knew God they did not accord him glory as God or give him thanks. Instead, they became vain in their reasoning, and their senseless minds were darkened. While claiming to be wise, they became fools and exchanged the glory of the immortal God for the likeness of an image of mortal man or of birds or of four-legged animals or of snakes.

Therefore, God handed them over to impurity through the lust of their hearts for the mutual degradation of their bodies. They exchanged the truth of God for a lie and revered and worshiped the creature rather than the creator who is blessed forever. Amen.

All of us lack the wisdom and discernment to know all of God's truths. But Paul explains very well that excuses do not exist to reject God and his truths. Paul notes that all of us who have reasoning powers have the ability to know God through his visible creations. Paul's words are of importance, when discerning other words our Lord spoke of blasphemy. In Paul's words he effectively is telling us that we blaspheme when we do "not accord him glory as God or give him thanks". Denying the existence of God is the greatest of all blasphemies.

It is important to all Christians to dwell on what our Lord had to say about blasphemy. Based on words our

Lord has spoken, I believe there is a connection that exists between blasphemy and hell.

Before turning to our Lord's words on blasphemy, it is also good to know that there are many spiritual definitions of blasphemy. We will spend time on some of those definitions as we go through this chapter.

Let us first look at what our Lord had to say regarding blasphemy in Matthew 12: 13&14: *Therefore, I say to you, every sin and blasphemy will be forgiven people, but blasphemy against the Spirit will not be forgiven. And whoever speaks a word against the Son of Man will be forgiven; but whoever speaks against the holy Spirit will not be forgiven, either in this age or the age to come.*

Because this chapter deals with Hell, let us first look at the unpardonable sin against the Holy Spirit. Jesus says this sin will not be forgiven, either in this age or the age to come. The highest degree of blasphemy is the very denial of the existence of God accompanied by that proclamation. It is my view that is the "blasphemy" of which Jesus speaks as being unpardonable. It is understandable, at least to me, that those who deny the very existence of God, are committing the sin that cannot be forgiven while that sin exists. In other words, one cannot reside in the Kingdom of God as long as one denies his very existence. However, if one converts and repents of that sin of blasphemy that sin no longer exists.

It is with caution that I believe what was just noted in the prior paragraph, because it is to some degree a personal discernment of what Jesus stated. Earlier,

I used words from St. Paul and he himself confessed to having been a blasphemer before his conversion. However, Paul did repent and convert and hence I believe his sin of blasphemy ended with that repentance and conversion. It is when that sin continues and remains ongoing, that it will not be forgiven. I should again state that opinion is based on my personal discernment. It is worth repeating that those who deny and proclaim that there is no God remain blasphemers.

Earlier, we noted that there are various definitions of blasphemy. Our Church provides some definitions of blasphemy in CCC 2148 of the Catechism:

Blasphemy is directly opposed to the second commandment. It consists in uttering against God inwardly or outwardly-words of hatred, reproach, or defiance; in speaking ill of God; in failing in respect toward him in one's speech; in misusing God's name...The prohibition of blasphemy extends to language against Christ's Church, the saints and sacred things. It is also blasphemous to make use of God's name to cover up criminal practices, to reduce peoples to servitude, to torture persons or put them to death. The misuse of God's name to commit a crime can provoke others to repudiate religion.

It is up to each of us to determine the gravity of sinful offenses caused by blasphemy. It is also up to each of us to discern the words He addressed as being blasphemous and unpardonable. As noted at the beginning of this chapter, many various views exist.

Let us now turn to what our Church has to say about Hell. The beginning section of Hell in the Catechism is CCC 1033, and it is as follows:

We cannot be united with God unless we freely choose to love him. But we cannot love God if we sin gravely against him, against our neighbor or against ourselves: "He who does not love remains in death. Anyone who hates his brother is a murderer, and you know that no murderer has eternal life abiding in him." (Parenthetical is from gospel of St. John) Our Lord warns us that we shall be separated from him if we fail to meet the serious needs of the poor and the little ones who are his brethren. To die in mortal sin without repenting and accepting God's merciful love means remaining separated from him forever by our own free choice. This state of definitive self-exclusion from communion with God and the blessed is called "hell".

Recently, I came upon someone's definition of blasphemy that was not too much different than those opening words in the Catechism; "Blasphemy against the Holy Spirit (the unpardonable sin) consists of progressive resistance to truth that ends in a final and irrevocable decision against it and involves a person choosing his own action in opposition to God's Word."

The common thread running through Biblical, Catechetical and other theological views on blasphemy and other serious threats to everlasting damnation is lack of love. That is also very logical, because God is love and Heaven will be a place where love abounds.

It is a personal belief of mine that human beings choose not to be in Heaven during their time on earth. Heaven would not be a place of eternal bliss for those who deny God's existence or those who despise or even reject his love and his commands. In that blasphemy they are simultaneously rejecting a place in his Kingdom. They are committing the unpardonable sin of which our Lord spoke in the gospel of Matthew. "We cannot be united with God unless we freely choose to love Him".

CHAPTER 13

HEAVEN – ETERNAL BLISS

The goal of every human being on earth should be to live eternally with our Lord in Heaven. But we are sinners and have frequent distractions in our efforts to achieve that goal.

If we wish to live our eternal life in bliss with our Lord, we need to prepare our souls in this life on earth and remember his words from Matthew 7 - 13&14; Enter *through the narrow gate; for the gate is wide and the road broad that leads to destruction, and those who enter through it are many. How narrow the gate and constricted the road that leads to life. And those who find it are few.*

In that passage our Lord tells us that it will not be easy during our time on earth to always live in a manner that "leads to life". We must make the observance of his two great commandments our top priorities while we are on earth. To be with Him in Heaven requires us to live a life of love of Him and our neighbors. Heaven is not a place for those who dwell on hatred and divisiveness in this life.

Love is a two-way street. There is no doubt that our Lord loves all his human creations, but to enter Heaven, He requires that our Love of Him and neighbors is at a level that allows us to be with Him and the saints. We simply would not fit into that eternal place of bliss, if our soul is not ready.

For those who wish to choose to "enter through the narrow gate" and live in accord with His commands, they will be rewarded with an eternal life which "eyes have not seen, and ears have not heard".

We do not know much about the Kingdom God has prepared for those who love Him, but in faith we know it will be a place that exceeds our expectations. It will be a place where love reigns supreme and where hatred and divisiveness do not exist. Eternal happiness will be a fulfillment for those who have lived as He wishes us to live.

While it is true that we know almost nothing of that bliss-filled Kingdom, we are given some insights in several books of Sacred Scripture and especially in the Book of Revelations.

In his letter to the Corinthians, St. Paul told us very succinctly that "there will be glory, honor and peace for everyone who does good". That glory, honor and peace will not be just for a few months or years, but for eternity. To live in His presence, should alone be a powerful incentive to live as He would have us live.

One of the Scriptural passages that provides some insight to the Kingdom of Eternal Love is in Chapter 21 of Revelation verses 1-7:

Then I saw a new heaven and a new earth. The former heaven and the former earth had passed away and the sea was no more. I also saw the holy city, a new Jerusalem, coming down out of heaven from God, prepared as a bride adorned for her husband.

I heard a loud voice from the throne saying, "Behold, God's dwelling is with the human race. He will dwell with them and they will be his people and God himself will always be with them (as their God). He will wipe away every tear from their eyes, and there shall be no more death or mourning, wailing or pain, for the old order has passed away.

The one who sat on the throne said, "Behold, I make all things new." Then he said, "Write these words down for they are trustworthy and true." He said to me, "They are accomplished. I am the Alpha and Omega, the beginning and the end. To the thirsty I will give a gift from the spring of life-giving water. The victor will inherit these gifts, and I shall be his God, and he will be my son.

But Revelation 21 also reminds us that the new heaven and new earth will not be a place for the unfaithful and those who have not lived a life that merits their place there.

It is only the foolish who do not believe in our God and eternal life. St. Paul in his letter to the Romans made it clear that through his creations God made it possible to know of his existence. Those with spiritual wisdom understand that. From his creations and the knowledge that He exists we can understand that He is divine. Once our faith accepts that reality, we can move on to meditate on what awaits us after death if we lead our lives on earth as our God wants us to live that life.

Relative to eternity, our life on earth is very brief, but during that time we decide our eternal fate. Through his Son, God has revealed to us what we need to do to be with Him after our life and trial on earth is over.

It is the spiritually wise persons who, through faith, accept that God has sent his Son to die on the cross for us. If they live their life as God wants it lived, they will have their eternal dwelling place with Him in his Kingdom.

We will conclude with the words noted earlier in this book and which our Lord spoke to his Apostles on the night before He died. *Do not let your hearts be troubled. You have faith in God; have faith also in me. In my Father's house there are many dwelling places. If there were not, would I have told you that I am going to prepare a place for you? And if I go and prepare a place for you, I will come back again and take you to myself, so that where I am you also may be.*

ABOUT THE AUTHOR

George E Pfautsch spent most of his working life as a financial executive for a major forest products and paper company. His final years at Potlatch Corporation were spent as the Senior Vice President of Finance and Chief Financial Officer.

Following his retirement, he began writing and speaking about the national morality he believes was intended for this nation by the founding fathers of the country.

He is the author of fourteen previous books that deal with the subjects of morality, justice and faith. He is the co-author of a book written by Melitta Strandberg, which is the story of her family's quest for freedom, before, during and after World War II. He is also the co-author of a book written by Leroy New, the "Guitar Wizard" of Branson, Missouri.

He is married to Dodi, his wife of 60 years. They have two children and four grandchildren.

Printed in the United States
by Baker & Taylor Publisher Services